la
act
+2

ESSEX HALL LECTURE, 1921

THE LOST RADIANCE OF THE CHRISTIAN RELIGION

L. P. JACKS, D.D., LL.D., D.Litt.

By L. P. JACKS, D.D., LL.D., D.Litt.

THE LOST RADIANCE
OF THE
CHRISTIAN RELIGION

BY

L. P. JACKS, D.D., LL.D., D.Litt.
Principal of Manchester College, Oxford

NEW YORK
GEORGE H. DORAN COMPANY

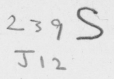

Copyright, 1924,
By George H. Doran Company

The Lost Radiance of the Christian Religion
— A —
Printed in the United States of America

PUBLISHERS' NOTE

THE Essex Hall Lecture was established with the object of providing an opportunity for the free utterance of the thoughts of a selected speaker on some religious theme of general interest.

The first lecture was delivered in 1893 by the late Rev. Stopford A. Brooke, on "The Development of Theology, as illustrated in English Poetry from 1780 to 1830." "The Relation of Jesus to His Age and Our Own," by Dr. J. Estlin Carpenter; "The Immortality of the Soul in the Poems of Tennyson and Browning," by Sir Henry Jones; "Heresy, Its Ancient Wrongs and Modern Rights," by the Rev. Alex. Gordon; "The Religious Philosophy of Plotinus, and

[v]

Publishers' Note

some Modern Philosophies of Religion," by
Dr. Inge, Dean of St. Paul's; "The Place of
Judaism among the Religions of the World,"
by Dr. Claude G. Montefiore; "Christianity
Applied to the Life of Men and of Nations,"
by Bishop Gore—these are a few of the subjects of the lectures in past years.

The lecture by Dr. L. P. Jacks on "The
Lost Radiance of the Christian Religion,"
when delivered, was warmly appreciated by
the audience, and it is believed that a wider
public will read it with interest.

ESSEX HALL, LONDON.

THE LOST RADIANCE OF
THE CHRISTIAN RELIGION

The Lost Radiance of the Christian Religion

OF all the interpretations of the Christian Religion there are few so false and none so worthless as those which reduce it to a wash of rose colour spread over the dark realities of the world, or to a group of fancies in which the soul of man, knowing them to be untrue, takes a deceitful holiday from the burden and the tragedy of life.

But while it is needful to guard ourselves against these sentimental perversions, of which there have been many, it is yet true that Christianity is the most encouraging, the most joyous, the least repressive and the least forbidding of all the religions of mankind. There is no religion which throws off the burden of life so completely, which escapes so swiftly from sad moods, which gives so large a scope for the high spirits of the soul, and welcomes to its bosom with so warm an embrace those things of beauty which are joys for ever. The Christian Religion has arduous phases; there are points on its onward path where it enters the deepest of shadows, and may even be said to descend into hell. But the end of it all is a resurrection and not a burial, a festival and not a funeral, an ascent into the heights and not a lingering in the depths. Nowhere else is the genius of the Christian Religion more poignantly revealed than in the Parable of the Prodigal Son, which begins in the minor key and gradually rises to the major, until it culminates in a great merrymaking, to the surprise of the Elder Son, who thinks the majesty of the moral law will be compromised by the music and the dancing, and has to be reminded that these joyous sounds are the keynotes of the spiritual world.

In our discussions of the religious needs of young people we are often tempted to regard Christianity as a religion of the old, which has by some means or other to be adapted to the minds of the young. I think we should be nearer the truth if we were to regard it as originally a religion of the young which has lost some of its savour by being adapted to the minds of the old.

In thus describing Christianity, I am thinking of its original genius; and not of the forms or the atmosphere it has acquired in the course of its chequered history, and in which it still survives. The chief difference (as it seems to me) between the original as we find it in the New Testament, and the forms with which we are familiar in our time, is that the modern version has lost the note of encouragement, and acquired again that very note of repression which has no place in the good news of Jesus Christ. There have been many corruptions of Christianity, and some of these, as we know, have damaged the innermost substance of its teaching. But perhaps the most serious corruption of all is not to be found in any list of the doctrines that have gone wrong. We find it rather in a change of the atmosphere, in a loss of brightness and radiant energy, in a tendency to revert in spirit, if not in terminology, to much colder conceptions of God, of man, and of the universe.

Indeed it is no uncommon thing to meet with persons of authority who openly avow that they are unable to sustain themselves in the atmosphere of the New Testament, that the only portions of it which appeal to them are those which fall into line with the stern obligations and straightforward moralities of the Hebrew religion, that all the rest is fantastic and artificial, and that they for their part are more at home in the Old Testament than in the New. To these persons it is matter of no moment when you tell them, in the language of St. Paul, that they are returning to the beggarly elements of the law; they attach little importance to what St. Paul says about these things; and their withers are unwrung. If you add that they are losing the radiance of Christianity, they answer "Let it go; it is more dazzling than useful; and we shall see better where we are when it is gone." Such an avowal is entitled to respect, if only for its honesty.

[13]

But there is another attitude of mind, far more common, which one can hardly respect quite as much. It belongs to those who have reverted without knowing it; who adopt the phrases distinctive of the Gospel, but miss the radiant energy that transfigures their meaning and makes them effectual; so that in the long run their Christianity reduces itself to the pursuit of moral excellence under a system of inviolable law, like the religion of the book of Deuteronomy.

The radiance of the Christian religion is a subtle and elusive thing which no definition can capture and no eloquence describe. It is not attached to any particular mode of presenting the doctrinal side. Christianity in its simplest and most intelligible form may be as deficient in radiance as any other. No doubt the simpler forms ought to retain it more easily than the complex. But that has not always happened. All that need be said is, that a simple Christianity which has lost its radiance is no more effectual than a complex Christianity under similar conditions. The simple like the complex may easily overlook the presence of a thing so subtle. In religion, as in art, the difference between the best and the second best is a difference that cannot be verbally formulated—"it is the matter of a hair, a shade, an inward quiver"—and yet what a difference it is! We recognize it in persons, though perhaps without knowing exactly what it is.

Indeed it was in the form of a person that the radiance of Christianity made its first appearance and its first impression on the world. It has a kinship with Beauty, but it stands for a Beauty so different from any other with which we are familiar that even that pregnant word does

[15]

not carry us very far. And yet it is no travesty of our religion to say that its power to move us lies in the vision it brings of a hidden beauty in the world, present even in the depths of pain and sorrow, and nowhere else so poignantly present as there, the sight of which is so encouraging, so invigorating, so exhilarating, that life and conduct are immediately raised to its own levels, and we ourselves become dispensers of it, with a new mastery over fate and circumstance, conquerors and more than conquerors over these light afflictions that are but for a moment. Christianity did more than tell us something new and refreshing about the nature of God. It told us something new and refreshing about the nature of the universe of which we are living parts. "A light came *into the world*"—so the Fourth Gospel puts it—not a light shed from without, but

[16]

a light that burns within the heart of the
world itself, transfiguring the whole length
and breadth of existence, from what it seems
to be to the eye of sense into the fullness of
its reality—the fitting abode of immortal and
rejoicing spirits, the Father's house of many
mansions, where music and dancing await
the regenerated soul, not only the music, to
which we listen, but the dancing which re-
produces the music in the total movement
of our lives. This is what I mean, and nothing less than this, when I speak of the radiance of the Christian religion—not an
adventitious quality, nor a mere alleviation
or adornment of an otherwise stern and un-
compromising code of duty, but an essential
and all-pervading energy, in which duty itself becomes a new creation along with
everything else, forgotten as duty because it

[17]

has been transformed into love, so that the poet could say:—

> Flowers laugh before thee on their beds,
> And fragrance in thy footing treads.

There are many ways in which we may read the New Testament; many moods in which we may respond to its appeal; many angles of vision from which we may interpret its teachings. Mostly we place it in an atmosphere which is certainly not its native air, and which it can hardly breathe without some loss of its essential radiance. How shall we describe the setting in which we most commonly place it? I am not using a veiled term of contempt when I call it the atmosphere of our Churches and Chapels. We read it in close connexion with the solemn exercises of religion and with the gravity of theological studies. We read it with the memory of endless controversies in

[18]

the background of our minds. We read it
as men who are anxious for the safeguard-
ing of morality, though the Gospel of
Christ is indeed no more anxious about
morality than it is about the morrow. We
read it as a portentous document which
brings us into the presence of dread alterna-
tives and bids us choose between life and
death. In such associations we naturally become pensive and our spirits apt to droop;
the light grows dim; the tone subdued; the
temper inelastic and sometimes perhaps a
little cowed. That is not a favourable state
of mind for penetrating the secret of Christ.
Our minds should be undisturbed by contro-
versial interests. There is that in the Gospel
which is more akin to the song of the sky-
lark and the babbling of brooks.

And yet I am far from saying that in all
this pensiveness we are utterly mistaken.

[19]

The Lost Radiance

There is room in Christianity for our pensive
moods. The compass of its theme is wide
enough to allow of many a passage in the
minor key, and perhaps even for a discord
here and there. There are moments indeed,
or phases when the whole meaning of our
religion seems to turn on the dark tragedy
of human existence; when Christ himself
comes before us a Man of Sorrows, and the
Cross overshadows everything else. But
these things are not dwelt upon in a heavy-
hearted way. Christianity does not brood
upon the sorrows of mankind. It is always
music that you hear, and sometimes dancing as well; and if at times the melody dies
out in a sad cadence, or even a cry of
despair, it is never final, but only the prelude
to a greater song. The mistake arises,
where we pitch upon the minor key as
though it were the characteristic note. This

[20]

I am afraid is what many of us have done; or shall I say what the church and chapel atmosphere has done for us; in spite of our knowledge that it is a misfortune. And the danger of it is great.

By approaching our religion exclusively from that point of view, by setting it exclusively in that atmosphere, we lose sight of the qualities which make it a religion of encouragement, until little by little it slips back to the very thing it was intended to supersede, becoming a system of repression, directed against a race of men who cannot be trusted, and who need the terrors of the law, veiled perhaps under a new terminology, to coerce them into obedience. Whenever that happens Christianity fails. It fails through the loss of its radiant energy. It sinks to the level of a philosophy of life piping to a world that will not dance.

The Lost Radiance

It is strange, after the Christian religion has been studied and practised for so many ages, though it has been studied far more than it has been practised, that we need to remind ourselves so often that Christianity is essentially the religion of the spirit. It was so to Jesus; it was so to St. Paul; and it should be so to us. The final object of a spiritual religion must always be the Spirit, that and nothing else. "God," said Jesus, "is Spirit," and it is a definition of God which goes behind and beneath all the other names that are applied to Him. And not only the object of it but the source; the well-spring of all motives, as well as the goal of all desires. The fruit of the Spirit, says St. Paul, is love, joy, peace, and the rest, all the great virtues following in the train of these three. These are the fruits of the spirit, because they are the

[22]

nature of the spirit. The spirit is love; it
is peace; it is joy; and perhaps joy most of
all. It is a joyous energy, having a centre
in the soul of man. It is not a foreign principle which has to be introduced into a man
from without; it belongs to the substance
and structure of his nature; it needs only to
be liberated there; and when once that is
done it takes possession of all the forces of
his being, repressing nothing, but transfiguring everything till all his motives and desires
are akindled and aglow with the fires and
energy of that central flame with its love, its
peace, its joy.

We are introduced to a conception of man
which represents him as a vast reservoir of
spiritual force, unused, undeveloped, perhaps even unborn, but waiting for liberation,
and destined when liberated to clothe him
with splendid virtues, to expand his being

[23]

over an enormous range, to make his garments whiter than any fuller on earth can white them, and his countenance to shine as the sun.

Over against this conception of man the Religion of the Spirit furnishes a conception of the world, of the universe, of reality, to correspond. As man in his innermost nature is a far higher being than he seems, so the world in its innermost nature is a far nobler fabric than it seems, precisely the kind of place, or of home, where the liberated spirit can find a never ending field for its activities, and a never ending theme for its joy. Man and his world are transfigured together; how could it be otherwise, seeing that both are of one substance? It is not man alone, but the whole creation, groaning and travailing in pain together until now, that stands to be delivered by the Spirit, de-

[24]

livered from the vision that is incomplete
into the vision that is complete, delivered
from the bondage of corruption into the glo-
rious liberty of the children of God. Such
is the compass and depth of the Christian
religion—the Religion of the Spirit. Such
are the qualities which make it pre-eminently
a religion of encouragement, and throw
it into sharp contrast with that other type
of religion, which preceded it and has
often usurped its place—the religion whose
keynote is *domination,* whose method is repression, whose atmosphere is gloom and
whose end is failure.

With these conceptions in mind let us read
our New Testaments again, asking ourselves
whether it really is the portentous document
the churches and chapels have made of it, or
rather whether the portentous elements,
which are assuredly there, are not themselves

[25]

so transfigured in the general transfiguration that they change their character and become radiant things along with all the rest.

Almost the first thing to greet us is an angel's song. To what is that the prelude? What does it lead us to expect? What is to be the nature of the symphony when the music begins in a theme so light hearted and jubilant? A new system of ethics, a corrected theology, an improved version of the Hebrew conception of God? Surely it is to be something more. And these weary and heavy laden souls whom Jesus invites into the haven of his rest. Who are they? Are they not chiefly ourselves, bowed down with moral anxieties, oppressed by the burden of a world whose nature we have thoroughly mistaken, blind to the eternal values of which it is the home, and sadly thinking that we were born to set it right.

[26]

The glory he saw in the flowers of the field, the infinite importance of the sparrow's fall, of the hairs of our head, of the two mites thrown into the treasury and of all the minute particulars of existence, the elemental joyousness that he loved in little children, the father's face which their angels rejoice to behold, the feast that crowns the turmoil of the Prodigal's life, the fruit of the vine that he will drink no more till he drinks it new in his father's kingdom, the paradise promised to the dying thief, the light come into the world of which the Fourth Gospel tells the story, the exuberant high spirits of the farewell discourses, the house of many mansions, the waving aside of death and tribulation as things that are overcome, the glory seen by St. Paul in the face of Jesus Christ and reflected in the liberty of the children of God,

[27]

and finally the New Jerusalem coming
down out of heaven from God, made ready
like a bride adorned for her husband—all
these, and much else of the same kind have
a deeper significance than our pensive
theologies have dared to find in them. They
are more than incidental—more than pleas-
ant resting places in a painful life of moral
endeavour, more than the bright moments
of a severe and sombre pedagogy. They
belong not to the fringe of Christianity but
to its essence. Their meaning is cosmic and
universal. They are the keys to the riddle
of life, prophecies of the end of all things,
revelations of the reality that abides beyond
the shadows, insights into the nature of that
spirit whom unless men worship, they worship not the God of Jesus Christ. And the
life of loving service, of imperturbable good
cheer, of high-hearted fellowship and gener-

[28]

osity, which blends with all this as the words of a song blend with the music to which they are set, is neither an introduction nor an appendix, but a natural response which the soul makes and cannot help making to a world built on the same heavenly pattern with itself and aglow with the same immortal fire.

I cannot but think that we are never further from the genius of the Christian religion than when we treat this luminous atmosphere as though it were a foreign envelope, of little account so long as the substance it enshrines is retained intact. Without it, the substance, no matter how simple or how complex, becomes a dry formula, dead as the moon. Losing the radiance we lose at the same time the central light from which the radiance springs, and our religion, instead of transforming the corruptible world into its incorruptible equivalents, reverts to the type it was intended to supersede and becomes a mere safeguard to the moral law.

Can a religion of this nature be translated into the homely terms of human conduct? Can it become the driving power of a noble life? Can it be applied to solving the concrete problems of our civilization? Can it be used as a master principle for building up the form of human society?

That the Christian religion has influenced our social life at many important points cannot be denied. That it has ever been used as the master principle of construction I greatly doubt. Indeed we have grown so accustomed to guiding our conduct by other ideals, and to solving our problems by other methods, and the mental habits that go with these have become so em-

[30]

bedded into the structure of our thought
that to many minds the Christian method
appears to be no real method at all. Nay
more. Convinced as most of us now seem
to be that human progress is mainly to be
won through the medium of political action,
we often imagine that we are appealing to
Christian principles when, as a matter of
fact, we are yielding to the very obsession
from which Christ lived and died to deliver
the world.

At all events, no one can view the pass
to which we are now come, the dreadful
confusion bordering on anarchy in which
the fortunes of mankind have become involved, without suspecting that great illusions have been at work, and feeling himself
challenged to think out the causes of these
things in the light of first principles. Such
an effort will not be in vain. It will be re-

warded by a threefold discovery; first, that the Christian principle still awaits its application at the central point; second, that the opportunity for applying it exists at the present moment; third, that nothing can allay these discords short of those radiant conceptions of God, of man, of the universe, which are the life and essence of Christianity.

Look at them once more. On the one hand there is the idea of man as a being of vast potentialities; from which it follows that the first need of man is not limitation but expansion, not repression but encouragement. Corresponding to this is the idea of the world as a storehouse of inexhaustible riches which man's nature befits him to appropriate and entitles him to enjoy. Suppose now that civilization, starting with the impulse given to it by those ideas, had followed them out step by step through the ages—what direction would the course of history have taken? Clearly the chief concentration of energy would have been on the "development" of this wonderful being, on what we may call the "education" of man's spirit in the largest sense of the term. All those methods, whether religious or political, would have been avoided which start from the assumption that man is either depraved or dangerous, and which, by assuming that he is depraved or dangerous, end by making him so. That is to say, many features which are now deeply characteristic of the social structure as we know it would never have come into existence. The schools would still be there, but the prisons would not. Equally impossible would have been the rise of a large number of powerful political States standing in perilous and warlike relationships to one another.

Negatively we can say this and a great deal more, ruling out, one by one, institutions and characteristics so closely linked with what we know as civilization that we can hardly think of civilization without them. This leaves it the more difficult to say positively what form society would have taken, had the aim throughout been the development of man. Power and domination, which are now the outstanding features, would certainly have become subsidiary, and might possibly have disappeared altogether. I have sometimes thought that we get a more positive hint, faint but significant, from existing groups and communities where education or development is the avowed object of the association. In the best of our schools and colleges, in certain aspects of University life, in the societies which exist for promoting the arts and sciences we have a type of human relationship which the imagination can easily extend to a world-wide scale. I do not suggest that the mission of Christianity was to turn the whole world into a school or college; but I do suggest that the spirit of fellowship and goodwill that is to be found in the best of these institutions is capable of producing a rich and varied type of social structure in the world at large. Conceivably it might have furnished the evolution of the west with its main motive and line of direction, with the result that we should be living in a world as unlike to the present as two things could possibly be.

But, as we know, civilization launched out in another direction. Instead of concentrating on development, as Christianity was inviting it to do, it concentrated on *gov-*

[35]

ernment. Unable or unwilling to grasp the truth that the first need of man is to be taught, the western world reverted to the legalist notion that man is a dangerous being, whose first need is to be governed—a being with whom you can do nothing till you have put a bridle in his teeth. Under the malign obsession of this belief everything was gradually pushed back to the point from which the religion of the spirit had pushed it forward—religion, theology, morals and politics—so that western civilization, hardly knowing what it did, again fell under the sway of ideas which were nothing more nor less than the old leaven of legalism under a new disguise. The universe itself was conceived as founded on a system of iron law which it is death to disobey, a conception which empties the world immediately of everything that makes it a home for the creative spirit. So deeply has this idea entered into the structure of our thought that to this day it is no uncommon thing to hear the laws of nature spoken of as though they were legal enactments,—to which they present not the least analogy.

In all this there was naturally involved a parallel degeneration in the idea of God. Men still spoke of him as the Father, following the terminology of Christ, but missing altogether its spirit. Under the stress of the surrounding ideas nothing could prevent the popular imagination from translating this term into the vision of a venerable potentate, a grandfather rather than a father, a patriarch rather than a companion, administering rewards and penalties under fixed statutes, and listening to the petitions of his subjects for their mitigation. God is light, God is love, God is Spirit—these phrases were still

[37]

repeated, but for the multitudes of mankind the life and the meaning was gone out of them.

The reaction on human conduct, on the structure of society, on the form of education was disastrous. Conduct took the form of submission to a law imposed from without, with the result that virtue lost its creativeness, while the mass of mankind became recalcitrant on the spot, government became domination, with the result that the dominating few became corrupt and the dominated many rebellious; education became the process of *breaking in* the spirit, with the result that only execeptional men could obey the call of their Maker by *breaking out*. Belief passed into dogma; the mind of man was put in fetters as well as his body; the Church built one prison and the State built another —the earthly counterpart of that eternal

[38]

prison where the monarch of the universe tormented the souls of his disobedient subjects for ever and ever. All this was closely connected with the idea of the *potentate God* which Church and State, in consequence of their political alliance had restored, against the martyr protest of Jesus Christ. Thinking of God in these degenerate terms, and hearing that they themselves had been made in his image, what more natural than that men should often think of themselves as little potentates, whose mission in life was to lay down the law for their fellows.

The ex-Kaiser of Germany is by no means a solitary instance of a man who fancied himself most like God when he was giving an order to his troops, that is to say, when he was least like God. In subtler but not less mischievous forms the same illusion has been at work for thousands of years, not only in the few who possessed authority, but in the multitudes who were anxious to possess it, and so turn the tables on their oppressors. I doubt if we have fully realized to what a degree the current ideas of God, of the world, and of the Divine Government have been moulded by habits of thought which have their origin in the peculiar needs of conquering races and war-making empires; nor do we see how these same ideas, reacting on the social conditions from which they spring intensify misunderstandings at every point and fill the world with ill-will, bad blood, inhuman delusions, and perpetual strife. Is it not a strange thing that century after century the history of our civilization in large affairs as in small, has turned on that forbidden question, "Who shall be greatest?"; a question which assumes Protean forms, but which, in its newest forms, as in its old-

[40]

est, is utterly alien to the Christian conceptions of man, and has no place whatever in the religion of the spirit. Hence that hideous struggle for power, that moves for ever in a vicious circle, now breaking out into terrific conflicts between nation and nation, now into class wars that are hardly less destructive, strewing calamity at every stage of its futile progress, until at last it brings the world to the verge of social and political anarchy.

The Dean of St. Paul's has recently stated that the problem of human government still remains unsolved. It remains unsolved because in and by itself it is insoluble. It becomes soluble only when placed in strict subordination to other questions that are far more vital than itself. Treat man, after the mind of Christ, as a being whose first need is for light, and whose second need is for gov-

ernment, and you will find that as his need
for light is progressively satisfied, his need
for government will progressively diminish.
That is the only solution of the problem of
government. Reverse the order, treat him as
primarily a subject, whether of God or king,
or demos, and what happens? The politics
of the world will tend towards chaos, as they
now are doing, while religion will decline
step by step until it becomes indistinguish-
able from the moral pedagogy, whose im-
potence has been demonstrated by innumer-
able failures. The struggle for power has
now involved the whole fabric of our civilization, and each new phase of its leaves the
final solution more remote and unattainable.
It is the inevitable consequence of reverting
to the idea of *domination,* as the key of God's
relation to man and of man's relation to his
fellows. On that ground the doom of man-

kind is perpetual strife. There is nothing
for it but to fight it out, and to go on fight-
ing it out, phase after phase, till civilization
has spent its resources and the higher ener-
gies of the race are exhausted.

But there are many hopeful signs; and
the chief of them all in my judgment is the
growing recognition, all over the world, that
man's primary need is for light. If the
Churches should be led by the Spirit of God
to ally themselves with this, the lost radiance
of the Christian religion will return, and the
Church will become the foremost teacher of
mankind. If not, the spiritual revival will
take place all the same; but it will take place
not in the churches but in the schools. In
the next generation there will grow up, there
is growing up even now, in this country and
in many others, a vast unordained ministry
of religion who will find their mission at the

teacher's desk. Along with this, there is a hunger for light in every class of the community which exceeds all existing means of satisfying it. Is it not a significant fact that while the churches are complaining of emptiness, the schools, the colleges, the universities, are packed to overflowing? Within the last few weeks I have met a Frenchman, a Swede, a Dutchman, an American, a Chinaman and a Japanese. To each I put the same question: "What is the leading interest in your country? What do your people really believe in?" And in each case the answer given was the same—Education. When I varied the question, and asked: "What have you learnt from the war?" the answer was: "We have learnt our need of education." Some would prefer them to have said: "We have learnt our need of Christianity." But is it not the same thing? In grasping the vast potentialities of the human spirit, and that is what this hunger for education means, have they not grasped an essential characteristic of the Christian religion, and placed themselves at its very growing point? Unless the signs are wholly misleading—and I cannot believe that they are —a movement has already begun, on the surface but more beneath the surface, which, if it develops according to promise, will grow into the most impassioned enterprise so far undertaken by man.

The struggle for *light,* with its wide fellowships and high enthusiasms, will displace the struggle for *power,* with its mean passions, its monstrous illusions and its contemptible ideals. Instead of Education being a department of Government as now, Government will become a department of Education. The struggle for power will end, not as some predict, in universal revolutions, which would merely set it going

[45]

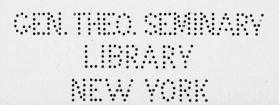

again in another form, but by being submerged, lost sight of, snowed under by the greater interests that centre round the struggle for light. I say these things will happen. But they will not happen unless men are sufficiently resolved that they shall. Already thousands are so resolved. Let us add our resolution to theirs, thereby taking the first step towards the recovery of the lost radiance of the Christian religion. For of one thing we may be assured. The struggle for light will not stop at a first series of discoveries. It will go on and on, from point to point, from position to position, from insight to insight, until the fruits of the Spirit are possessed, the eternal values revealed, the unsearchable riches laid bare, the many mansions fully opened, and the turmoil of life transfigured and explained in the music and dancing of an immortal world.

[46]